MODERN MYSTICISM

AND OTHER ESSAYS

First Edition 1910
Francis Grierson

New Edition 2020
Edited by Tarl Warwick

COPYRIGHT AND DISCLAIMER

FOREWORD

Francis Grierson is an interesting character within the literature of his era, interested in poetry, music, and of course, the mystic and occult; this work fuses those together, and much of its content is about the form and nature of various art forms (music, prose, poetry, plays, etc) and comparisons of the skill and mystic content of different names of note within each subgenre of creative material; as with most mystical minds interested in these subjects, for example, he applauds Shakespeare and Goethe, Wagner and Beethoven, among many others.

Informed in part by the tenuous nature of geopolitics at the dawn of the twentieth century, Grierson takes up a definitively pro-French and pro-American sentiment here, preferring the work of both general schools to those of England and Germany in specific, and noting that work from Russia often echoes the vast and un-endearing landscape of the steppe there. At times this leads him to wax political or even derisive of some works, but his analysis is, at least, usually even handed and always deep and meaningful. Mostly, he avoids too much mention of the more superficial, outright inclusions of spiritual topics in the analyzed works, and dwells more on the human psyche and the interplay between genres.

This edition of "Modern Mysticism" has been carefully edited for format and content. Care has been taken to retain all original intent and meaning.

MODERN MYSTICISM

PREFACE

Some years ago, while living in Paris, I persuaded the author of this volume to publish an opuscule of aphorisms and short essays in French. That little book, not being intended for the general public, was neither advertised nor put on sale. It was without introduction of any kind, and was printed by an obscure publisher. Worse still, it was printed in such haste as to be full of typographical errors. Notwithstanding all this, a few weeks after its appearance the author received some scores of letters from leading French writers and poets, among whom were many Academicians. But perhaps more remarkable still was the appreciation with which it was received by writers so opposed as M. Sully Prudhomme, of the French Academy, and M. Stephane Mallarme, the leader of les Jeunes. The former wrote of "l'originalite puissante de la pensee de l'auteur," and the latter of the "rare emotion" inspired by these pages.

A distinguished Italian critic, Signor Enrico Cardona, published a brochure on the little work, in the opening lines of which he defines Mr. Grierson as "un filosofo dal cuore di artista," thus making the author's name known in Italy.

Dona Patrocinio de Biedma, the well-known Spanish poet and writer, translated the aphorisms and most of the short essays, and published them in several of the leading journals of Spain.

In writing to the author, M. Maurice Maeterlinck said: "Let me tell you what joy it has been to me to encounter in your book a soul so strangely fraternal, perhaps I ought to say the most truly fraternal that I have yet found. You have deliciously and profoundly surprised me- you have said so many things which I should like to have written myself."

The author has made prolonged residences in the principal capitals of the world, and has had exceptional opportunities for the study of art and of human nature in every sphere of artistic and social life. The pages on Tolstoy and on Wagner are the result of a year's residence in Russia and a sojourn of several months in Bayreuth.

L. W. T.

MODERN MYSTICISM

Mystical inspiration is the essential element that assures immortality to any work, whether in poetry, art, music, or philosophy. Of all the forms which inspirational thought may take, that which is coeval with the art-form is the most vital and the most beautiful, because the most mystical. The highest inspiration demands the union of art and wisdom; and modern mysticism is both broader and deeper than that expressed in medieval times, for the wisdom of the past was often weakened by dogma and nullified by impracticable ideals. But even in ancient times the most consoling sentiments and the most sublime ideas were expressed in the artistic mold.

Job was a prose poet, Plato a poetic philosopher. The perennial charm of the book of Job lies in the fact of the sentiment and the language being conceived as one. Wisdom may be profound, but obscure thought cannot contain the highest wisdom. The best art, therefore, can be symbolical or allegorical, but the idea must be clear and the form evident. And as the mystical law demands the unity of thought and form, the same law stamps every new artist and poet with the seal of originality. They may borrow from one another, but they do not imitate. Inferior grades of inspiration are often engendered by preceding examples, but the possessor of an original faculty arrives with something indefinable. We recognize the charm, but we cannot explain it. We may call this power a "temperament," anything, indeed, except what is meant by the old-time definition of "special instrument for a special mission," which scientific knowledge of the present day forbids us to consider tenable. For, since we are all the result of ancestral forces, and conditions, to apply the term "instrument" to a human soul, capable of thinking and suffering, is to strip the mind of every vestige of personality and responsibility. It would reduce all forms of talent to a condition of inspired idiocy. Although this faculty has come into existence through a soil that has been plowed and harrowed by others, it now produces a new flower or a new fruit.

Modern mysticism is not only anti-provincial, it is anti-dogmatic as well. "L'esprit replie sur lui-meme," says M. Maeterlinck, "n'est qu'une celebrite locale qui fait sourire le voyageur." This is why genius, which is antithetical to local sentiment, is never typical of one race or nation. The Shakespeare of Hamlet is the most un-English of all our poets. The fundamental element of his inspiration is catholicity, and this could not exist were the poet swayed by provincial sentiment, passion, and reason. In like manner, Dante, Michelangelo, Beethoven, Goethe, to name but a few, were not representative types of their respective countries. Such minds rise clear above the local idea. They are universal because their thought is mystical and not methodical. It would be difficult to imagine anything more opposed to English sentiment than the mysticism displayed in Shakespeare, and yet there never was a time when the poet was so deeply appreciated by English thinkers nor so fully understood by Continental critics. The real man is the interior man; the superficial man has a provincial mind, he is warped by exterior influences. He revolves in a circle in which he believes himself developing and progressing; he is therefore often powerful in his own sphere, but his power is conventional and his influence ephemeral.

There is but one universal mode of thought, that of interior consciousness freed from schools and systems. We may or may not know more than the ancients, but the soul of man is certainly the same now as it was in the days of Solomon and Socrates. The exterior has changed, local forms of thought are more varied, but the man who wishes to think deeply must be prepared to think freely. The distance of the nearest fixed star can scarcely be conceived by the human mind, and the distance of the farthest, measured by mechanical means, passes beyond the province of human will and human imagination.

MODERN MYSTICISM

In this illimitable realm of mystery the mind perceives but does not comprehend; it gropes its way in infinite space; it can form no just idea of the fathomless ocean of ether in which we exist, revolving, as we do, a mere speck around a sun that is another speck in the stupendous sea of worlds.

No sooner does intuition penetrate to a new conception of Nature's enigma than the mind becomes conscious of revolving within a new circle of unsolved problems. Paradox and illusion are the riddles, the tempters, and the tormentors of poets and thinkers, for the deeper the soundings the more imperative the mystery. With all our systems and conventions the secret essence of the mind can no more be forced into fixed grooves now than in the olden times. With all our progress in mechanical invention and social comfort, the soul refuses to conform to exterior conditions, customs, influences, and examples. While the body goes its own way, passing from one grade of life to another, the mind has its own mode of progress, unknown to superficial observers.

And while we no longer dress, eat, and live like the ancients, we nevertheless think in similar moods and reason by similar methods. This is the immortal part of us. The mystical element in man today is as real and perennial as the mysticism of Athens and Jerusalem. The transmission of intuitive lore from one thinker to another is never direct and consecutive; the line of thought is broken at certain periods. Nature ordains these gaps, so that receptive minds may have time to appropriate certain fundamental maxims before a new thinker arises to solve one more riddle in the chaos of doubt and disorder.

Emerson followed Novalis without being his successor, but Emerson prepared the way for Maeterlinck, who, in his turn, reintroduces Novalis as one would present a newly discovered thinker to the notice of minds prepared to listen and comprehend. Novalis is a philosophical pagan, a metaphysical Christian, a scientific mystic. In many respects he is in German what Emerson is in English. Perhaps the principal charm of Novalis is his freedom from dogma; he never preaches. Such writers appeal only to readers capable of receiving light from within. Emerson was optimistic, utilitarian, democratic. More practical than poetic, he appeared at a time when new social conditions engendered new forms of thought, in a country where there was no special field for the propagation of poetic sentiment, and when art, in its purest phases, was a foreign and uncongenial element. Nevertheless, Maeterlinck is right when he places Emerson among the mystics; for, as the Belgian poet says, "Il y a mille mysticismes divers."

While Emerson is wise in the worldly sense, the wisdom of Novalis attains the metaphysical; it soars to heights which often make immortality incomprehensible and earthly existence unsatisfactory. He carries us to such altitudes that gazing upwards is unpleasant and looking below dangerous. But if Novalis often soars beyond the clouds, when he speaks of mind and personality he illuminates certain mysteries with incomparable flashes of wisdom. When he defines genius as the possession of the "rhythmic sense," we instinctively accept the definition as the most concise and lucid ever given of that inscrutable faculty. This rhythmic sense embraces the unity of thought and emotion, all that is architecturally harmonious in the mind, all that is poetic and psychological in the heart.

The best poetry, art, and music emanate from a source that contains the essential elements of universal science. Indeed, this harmony is the highest expression of the mystical element obtainable by the human mind. Errors in judgment and in art are caused by a denial or ignorance of the law of ethical and aesthetic correspondence. For, without a clear conception of the absolute relation of thought and art, even what the world accepts as serious work is rejected later as ephemeral.

MODERN MYSTICISM

BEAUTY AND MORALS IN NATURE

"La nature est d'une insensibilite absolue, d'une immoralite transcendente."

-Renan.

Nature takes no account of the ethical idea in the social economy of man. She is indifferent to everything except the struggle for life and beauty. But in the struggle towards the beautiful there is no moral aim.

Some of the most beautiful flowers contain the most virulent poisons, while beautiful faces more often denote stupidity and egoism than goodness and wisdom. Nature is a sensual force, which, as Amiel says, is "sans pudeur et sans probite." From the beginning she has striven for an expression of beauty, whether wise or ignorant, malignant or beneficent; and this principle lies at the base of the whole idea of creation, the one force acting in, through, and over all, ignoring the ethical idea developed by man, unconscious of his religious sentiment, blind to the scruples of civilization, indifferent to the moral code and the moral character. What nature was and is in the plane of matter she continues to be in the sphere of the mind. Personal beauty is as potent today as it was at the courts of Solomon and Pericles. Place a beautiful woman of ordinary intelligence beside a number of celebrated women with plain features, and note the difference between the sensation created by comeliness and the respect paid to the celebrities! In the daily battles waged between beauty and morals, the moralists are nearly always out-generaled; for the principle of beauty is a fundamental, changeless element in the order of the universe, while moral codes and notions belong to man, differing according to religion and custom.

MODERN MYSTICISM

Nature is inexorable in her multiple moods and methods. She laughs at systems and sermons, and while the preacher thinks his people well under discipline, there, right under his nose, the subtle charm is taking effect, the power of beauty, the immutable central soul cause is destroying old conditions and creating new ones, ignoring the precepts of the moralist and every maxim imbibed since childhood, to revel in the illusion which the magician Nature has conjured up from the fountain of infinite life.

In its influence beauty is suave or terrible, conciliating or contradictory, insensible or comforting. Preach at it, and it becomes a nightmare; reason it away, and it returns under new devices; accept it scientifically, and it becomes natural; accept it artistically, and it becomes a benediction; accept it philosophically, and it becomes a fundamental necessity. It mocks those who deny it and bites like a viper those who scorn it; its victims are those who blindly court it; its favorites are those who meet it as a friend. The materialist sees and enjoys principally the physical charm of beauty; the idealist responds mainly to its psychical quality; but its real power and mystery lie in the myriad expressions and combinations of the physical united with the psychical. And this is the one thing about personal beauty which eternally mystifies and surprises: every new face is a law unto itself The enthusiast who thinks he has mastered the secrets of form by familiarity with one or several types, falls an easy victim to his own naivete. Faces and forms are of infinite degree, like the stars; and like the stars, too, each type of beauty has its peculiar atmosphere, aeriform envelope, transparent or opaque, behind which the essence rolls and revolves under immutable and mysterious Law. The form is but the mask of the soul, be the soul wise or ignorant, subtle or naive, and familiarity with beauty implies contact with the psychical element that lies hidden behind the exterior. It is this dual quality which makes beauty twofold in its power; it not only attracts by its special form, but it enchants by the indefinable quality of its psychic principle. This is why beauty, in its most positive manifestation, is the most potent friend and the greatest enemy with which man has to deal. Beauty is more a danger to the sensitive idealist than it is to the sensual materialist, for the first is too impressionable to hold it within reasonable limits, and the second too practical to fall its victim. Bacon says, "There is no excellent beauty that hath not some strangeness in the proportion." This is so because the charm of all excellence is originality, just as art becomes a real thing when it rises above imitation. But Bacon errs when he says, "The principal part of beauty is in decent motion," for its chief virtue is in form, its second in mind, its third in motion. A graceful bearing is a potent charm when coupled with a handsome face without mind or when united to intellect, but simple grace of movement, although a charm in itself, is never so fascinating as beauty of feature and form. Every age has its special types of beauty as well as its special manifestations of genius, and, indeed, beauty and genius are the only forces in the social universe which make their own laws and compel us, consciously or unconsciously, to follow them.

But the tyranny of a beautiful woman with a callous heart is more fatal in the ranks of genius than is tyrannical genius in the ranks of nations. An Italian Aspasia or a French Cleopatra might have turned Bonaparte into a second Mark Antony and Boulanger into a second Bismarck. It is a mere hazard of Nature that couples a sweet disposition with extreme beauty. For beautiful women, like men of genius, are often what Cicero said of Pompeii, *sui amantes sine rivali*, the egoistic poison sometimes inherent in these two expressions of human nature equaling in virulence that of certain flowers whose perfume intoxicates and whose essence kills.

The chief danger of beauty is in the surprise which it creates. The mind of man can never conceive nor predict what fresh type will seize his imagination on a given day, at a certain hour; for, as in war the greatest danger lies in surprises, in society the greatest peril Hes in that kind of love inspired by wonder and admiration. There is nothing more fatal. When the foe has descended upon a sleeping camp, the most astute general is compelled to accept the consequences. Man receives with caution surprises that spring from political, religious, and scientific sources; and innovations are only effective when brought about by degrees; but he is rarely equipped to meet the quintessential forces of beauty revealed suddenly.

Of the two most sinister forms of beauty, the one devours by aggression, the other deceives by feints. This second is like an eternal mirage in the void of the human mind, and has led as many heroes to destruction as ever fell in battle. The forces of Nature build and destroy by the same element, and the tragedies that occur in the deserts of the imagination, through the fatal allurements of beauty, are, for the most part, never known; for men will confess to any loss or disappointment except that caused by the enticements, the stratagems, and the sorrows of chimerical love.

Envy usually anathematizes the things it most hates, and if comeliness could be extinguished by envy, the world would soon be without personal attraction in any form. The envy caused by beauty is at once more restricted and more bitter than that caused by genius; but as genius over-rides and neutralizes envy by a natural process of time and superiority, beauty acts like a magical antidote to malicious jealousy; it suffices to make itself visible and the reaction occurs, the thing is done; and, like all performances of magic, no one can tell precisely how the thing is done. Philosophers and wits have racked their brains in every age to unravel the enigma- the natural magic of a beautiful face defies analysis. There are no written codes to unravel the secret devices of Nature- they are unfathomable.

Cynics may continue to depose this or that queen of

beauty by a hon mot, by a contemptuous remark, by vulgar jests about a woman's age; but, with grace and intelligence, beauty can go a surprising distance before it ceases to charm; for beauty, even in age, is a power to be reckoned with; there are grandmothers living who, at the present moment, are being courted by the clever sons of their former playmates, and hundreds of wise men prefer the beauty of maturity to that of youth, recognizing in age a special and superior enchantment. And here, again, personal attraction resembles genius in its action on individual minds; no man, at liberty to decide for himself, has ever been influenced by envy against any particular type of what he considers beautiful; thus the potential quality of beauty is a silent resolvent; the charms of a wicked woman, like the charms of a good woman, render her enemies ridiculous by contrast and pitiable by the opposition of so much power to so much weakness.

In the life of the artist who has observed long and patiently the objectively beautiful is a constant friend and comforter. He has met beauty half-way, and held a parley with the arch-enemy, first with courageous humility, then with diplomatic audacity, and lastly on terms of equality; for, with the true artist, intimacy with beauty is the only kind of familiarity which does not lead to contempt; the artist respects the foe turned to friend, knowing that beyond familiar knowledge there lies a region of undefined mystery and charm, which, like the empyrean, is illimitable.

THE TRAGEDY OF MACBETH

An Imaginary Dialogue Between Euripides and Aeschylus

EURIPIDES: Concerning tragedy, I may say that the psychological law of simplicity in connection with that of illusion must be strictly observed in every part of it. In tragedy, as in all the realm of poetry, as well as in the higher philosophy, it is the simplest illusions that strike most deeply into the human heart; and in Macbeth it is these elements of illusion and simple poetic truth that carry the mind captive, charm the heart, and bewilder the imagination with vague personages, ideas, conditions, and objects. But when there is much noise, loud speech, intense action, confusion, and pomp of words, without the veil of suggestion which should always shroud the figures of tragedy, there can be little inspiration, little enthusiasm, and no mystery.

I will tell you why I regard Macbeth as the greatest tragedy the world has yet seen: it contains more mystery, illusion, and simplicity than any other work of the kind in any language. For does not mystery bewilder us? Does not illusion fascinate us? And does not simplicity win our sympathies and lodge in our understanding?

AESCHYLUS: I see clearly, as you have said, that there must be illusion and mystery in every great tragedy, also do I assent to the need of simplicity, both in the action and in the dialogue; but I think there should be more mystery, coupled with illusion, than simplicity in the action; for do not the two great tragic elements of love and murder require this?

EURIPIDES: In the action there should always be that train of thought which carries the mind captive, leading it on and on from one stage of the plot to another, proceeding slowly by a certain law of augmentation, which in tragedy, poetry, and music is always to be observed. But passing into the mysteries of tragic emotion, as in Macbeth^ is like the exploring of dangerous regions by night, where every step is uncertain as you grope your way in the deep shadows or deeper darkness, descending lower and lower, until terror and mystery unite as one.

AESCHYLUS: I must confess you give me new light on this subject, for I begin to see what you really mean by "mystery." This is truly the predominant trait of the greatest tragedies in which the depths of passion are reached. You have expressed it well, and I now see it more clearly than before. But tell me, what is the actual difference, in your opinion, between mystery and illusion in such a tragedy as Macbeth?

EURIPIDES: Mystery is the counterpart of illusion; the one may be compared to the caterpillar, the other to the butterfly; and in this I speak not only physically but spiritually; for the caterpillar is a mystery in that it suddenly changes, as it were, from beast to bird. And is not the butterfly an illusion to the sense of sight, as it darts here and there among the flowers and through the air, delighting the beholder by its rapid flight and brilliant colors? This is what illusion does to the mind; it flits before the senses like a phantom; but it is impalpable, it cannot be fully grasped by any of the senses; it has the elements of the real and the unreal. And so, too, has mystery, which is always filled with dim uncertainty, like a great cave that is never completely illuminated, but presents the alternations of flickering lights and dark shadows to those travelers who venture to look in at its mouth.

I will now explain why the tragedy of Macbeth is so filled with these elements, especially with illusion and mystery, according to their technical use in the drama. We have these in the characters both of Macbeth and Lady Macbeth. The banquet scene is an illusion combined with mystery, as the spirits come and go before the eyes of Macbeth, but are unseen by all the others. This seeming fantasy of the sense is a mystery to those beholding it, as well as to Macbeth himself, being, moreover, awful and overwhelming in its abruptness; and overall there soars the fatal chimera, flattering his vanity by the lips of his lady, for it is this that urges him on and on till the culminating point is reached. Certainly in no other drama have mystery and illusion been so effectively portrayed. We see it, indeed, in the beginning of the drama. As the first act opens out before us there seems to be an air of expectation hanging like a thin veil over it, through which we can almost see to the end the mighty scenes that are to follow.

AESCHYLUS: What part in the action, or what bearing upon the illusion or mystery in this great tragedy, has the music as sung by the witches?

EURIPIDES: Now, indeed, do you touch upon a vital point in Macbeth; one in which the illusive and the mysterious join hands and become as one, where the action brings with it all the results which naturally flow from such causes. We see depicted before us, not only to the physical sense of sight and to the sense of melody, but in a psychological aspect, the distinctly mystical quality of the conception when we hear the witches sing and see them dance, coming, as they do, in that particular part of the tragedy, neither too soon nor too late, but at the exact point where all is adjusted to a harmony that is as wonderful as it is fascinating. We see them before us dancing and singing and exulting over something, we hardly know what; but we feel that it is something of vital significance; and, let me say, the music itself heightens the effect of the whole action. The man who composed it must have had a clear conception and a deep appreciation of the peculiar elements of this tragedy.

As for subtleties, Macbeth is full of them; and yet, strange to say, it is one of the simplest works ever written. For the charm of illusion is simplicity, by which it takes us captive, like the face of a beautiful woman when smiling, who says nothing, but leaves all to the suggestive fancy of the beholder. Not as the world understands it is Macbeth subtle. To the unobserving, to the mind unaccustomed to analyze, it would be very difficult to appreciate the glories of such a work, its motive, its action, and its influence. And touching the scene of the witches, I will say that no lover of Shakespeare, no tragedian with a due appreciation of his art, will ever permit this tragedy to be presented without the full musical score.

AESCHYLUS: And now tell me what, according to your understanding, is the most illusive, the most mysterious, the most suggestive, and yet the simplest passage in Macbeth.

EURIPIEDES: This question would seem to be a very difficult one, since it appears to embrace a review of the whole drama; but it is, in fact, quite simple, for it can be answered in a few words. In that great scene, at once vivid and sublime, just after the murder, when Macbeth is shrouded in the gloom of psychological mystery, awe, and terror, mingled with vanity, ambition, and the prospect of glory, he asks the question, "Didst thou not hear a noise?" And, amid the brooding silence, Lady Macbeth replies, "I heard the owl scream and the crickets cry." In this scene are combined all the elements of mystery, illusion, and simplicity. It suggests to the cultured mind the principles of the highest tragic colloquy. I deem that passage the most transcendent in all the work of Shakespeare; nor has it a parallel in the work of any other poet. What weirdness is there! The solemn stillness of night, the ominous screech of the owl, the cricket's plaint, from some remote crevice, following the night-bird's scream like a warning from an invisible witness, the medieval castle, the two beings, impelled by inexorable ambition to the murder of the King- these things occasion the most suggestive passage in the whole realm of tragedy! As to the knocking at the door, which a great writer has spoken of as involving the reaction of noise and confusion after the murder, I admit its effect is powerful, but the conception is not poetic, for in these knockings the reaction is material; the incident suggests a return to ordinary life after the commission of the deed, and the effects of it have no metaphysical bearing upon the progress of the play.

AESCHYLUS: And what, may I ask, is the difference between Greek tragedy and Macbeth?

EURIPIDES: There are many differences, both in the conception and in the action. While, in the Greek tragedy, we find much of the subtlety which was congenial to the Greek mind, with the weirdness of fatal sorrows growing out of the calamities which befall the chief personages in the drama, there is not that simplicity which is so striking a feature in Macbeth, and which makes it so potent in its influence on the imagination and the feelings. The Greeks were masters of a few of the elements of tragedy. What they attempted they accomplished with a wonderful degree of perfection; but their works were lacking in the elements of illusive suggestion, and above all in that simplicity or truthfulness to Nature which is so prominent throughout Shakespeare's tragedies.

To be thrilling in its effect on the mind, to be fascinating, to be illusive yet real, a tragedy- and indeed every great poem, dramatic or epic- must proceed by grades, passing, as in a symphony, from major to minor and back again, exalting the mind, thrilling the nerves with strong emotions, pleasing the imagination with new fancies, augmenting the movement by changes, until a climax is reached, which, in the catastrophe of the drama, concentrates in one scene all the elements of ambition, mystery, and emotion.

MODERN MELANCHOLY

Modern melancholy has, before everything else, its gesture. Its natural motion is the gesture of disillusion, a weary, languid mien of abandonment. What resignation there is in its most typical phases! For the spirit of disenchantment is ennui, and fatigue is anti-dramatic. And so is the acting of Madame Yvette Guilbert. She expresses abnormal emotion by normal methods. Her art is the synthesis of modern pessimism and disillusion. It contains weird suggestions of passing chimeras, vague reminiscences of vanished dreams, vivid reality and poignant simplicity.

The medieval attitude of melancholy was that of faith and resignation. The characteristic of the sadness of our age is dejection, often accompanied by indifference and unwillingness to enunciate. Disenchantment can only be expressed by the three moods of poetry, music, and gesture. And gesture is the most congruent expression of the soul, therefore the most apparent. The beggary and misery of the suppliant at the street corner is shown by attitude first of all, then by facial expression, and lastly by intonation. And if the natural form of disillusion is one of mute dejection, it is the antithesis of pantomime with its imbecile extravagance and affected emphasis. The very effort of pantomime puts a damper on imagination and feeling.

The basic element of Madame Guilbert's art is quietude; she stands before us, not in a theatrical robe, but in a modern gown, without stage illusions, devoid of theatrical method or style. The French *diseuse* is a spontaneous revelation of what many poets, artists, actors, and musicians of our time have felt but have never succeeded in expressing. Without this attitude the poetry of modern disenchantment is mere intellectual suggestion, and the melancholy of modern music never surpasses a sentimental semblance of emotional reality. Madame Bernhardt shows us how a classical method, with its measured inflections, its aristocratic reticence, and varied attitudes can develop dramatic art. Madame Guilbert's art is a spontaneous conception, a creation in the highest sense of the word. All dramatic art, properly speaking, is evolved from experience and imitation. She sprang forth as in a night, like a tragic apparition denuded of the paraphernalia of tragedy. And yet, by the gesture of two long phantom-like arms, by the listless posture of a statuesque neck, by the languid roll of the eye, by a peculiar inimitable movement of the shoulders, she suggests and depicts a world of ideas, passions, emotions, illusions, both poetic and commonplace. She invokes the everyday sentiments and sensations that lie beyond mere words and phrases. Her art is never vehement. It is smothered passion. It is the fire of love covered with the ashes of disillusion. And yet it is not acting; it is simple, unsophisticated gesture. Nor does she sing, properly speaking; nor does she need to sing. Her features announce what is too deep for words, and her voice intones what lies beyond the realm of musical phrasing.

We had in the Pre-Raphaelite movement the art-romance of modern melancholy; we have the poetic sentiment of it in the dramas of Maeterlinck; we have in Wagner's Lohengrin, and Tannhauser the musical emotion of it. In all this one moves in the realm of the highest art, and it is more or less metaphysical. For these masters express modern sadness and disillusionment by ideal efforts and effects. The impression produced belongs more to the spiritual than to the worldly plane of life; we are carried over and beyond ordinary existence, sentiment, and feeling. What we call the grand art of the poets and painters carries us away, leaving us no time to stop and think. It is real in the spiritual sense. It is beauty and hope in Burne-Jones, beauty and longing in Rossetti, beauty and despair in Maeterlinck, beauty and madness in Wagner.

In presentations such as *La Soularde* and *La Morphinee*

MODERN MYSTICISM

Madame Guilbert puts us face to face with what is. She lifts the curtain and we see the ghastly fact. There are no limelights.

There are no cadences, no illusive settings, nor woven fancies. We are placed suddenly beyond the lamentations and the vaguely cherished dreams even of the most pessimistic poets, and we stand before the pine coffin of Hope covered with the faded roses of modern disillusion. The time is past for weeping, and gesture has taken the place of tears; it is all that art can do, not at its lowest, but at its last and final stage. Although realistic, it is too reticent to be brutal. Nor is it limited to one sphere of modern life. It comprises a vast social world, from the cynical despair of Montmartre to the sentimental despair of the Madeleine. The first is a frank confession of a glaring social fact; the second, a religious and secret confession of the same troubled state of the soul. This art is not only a Latin and Parisian development; all nations understand it, for the language and gesture of modern melancholy are universal.

TOLSTOY

The portrait of Tolstoy denotes pride and will; the portrait of Rousseau, sensibility and originality. Tolstoy is an aristocrat who has sought peace in plebeian humility. Rousseau was a provincial sentimentalist who began his career by seeking the society of philosophers. The expressions in these two faces tell the story of conflicting emotions and intellectual paradox ending in mental disorder.

Tolstoy mistakes mere humility for religion, and poverty for progress. The French writer caused a revolution of ideas; the Russian wishes to cause a revolution of deeds as well as of ideas. When Rousseau wrote his Confessions, he united emotional fantasy with psychological observation; while Tolstoy leaves the domain of sane talent and healthy art for a sphere of eccentric experimentation. There is a wide gap between a pensive temperament and a morbid imagination. The one is marked by philosophical harmony, the other overflows with vague visions of perfectibility.

But the celebrated Russian has not developed that spirit of humility which some writers would have us believe. Indeed, his *pronunciamientos* are not so much the result of humility as of malicious rivalry; for when he asks Englishmen to give up Shakespeare, Germans to give up Beethoven, Italians to give up Dante, it is, of course, with the express understanding that Count Tolstoy shall take their place. The teaching of this writer calls to mind the old error, taught in different forms in all ages, of the possible attainment of intellectual and moral equality. If such men would calmly contemplate the heavens by night and note the difference in the size and glory of the stars, or walk into the woods to take lessons from the beasts and the birds, all differing in form and color, they would see that the physical structure of the universe conforms to the spiritual and moral faculties of man in that both harmonize with the universal and immutable law of variation and inequality.

Instead of a manifestation of genius we have in Count Tolstoy a depressing sense of will-power, unbalanced by culture and intuition. It is literary Nihilism put into practice by a converted pessimist.

After reading books like the Kreutzer Sonata and La Bete Humaine, one is tempted to ask what these painful recitals do towards the elevation of art or humanity. The artist and the thoughtful reader answer this question by comparing such books with the work of Scott and Balzac. The work of the modern realist is the art of fact, comparable to problems in algebra. Literary realism is artistic materialism, the pugilism of intellectuality. The disciples of realism tell us that there is a profound and practical philosophy in this kind of writing; but the realities of everyday life are sufficiently vivid to permit of dispensing with this new form of modern emotion. Think of an age of practical research being called upon to supply a literature of physical suffering and psychological sorrow, to harmonize, as it were, with the doubts of a Spencer and the dynamics of a Darwin! It is not surprising that a large number of persons daily seek refuge in phenomenal mysticism when one considers the psychological inquisition to which readers of novels have been put during the past twenty years.

The study of Tolstoy means the study of Russian character, with its superstitions, its contradictions, its strange medley of fanaticism and pessimism. This character is strongly tinctured with Oriental mysticism, coupled with a new form of Western thought. The Russians imitate much, create little. In this soil theories take root with singular facility. Character distinguishes one man from another, and gives identity; true personality distinguishes one man from all others, and gives originality. Every human being that lives a sober, industrious life possesses character, but neither sobriety nor industry will give personality. The quality of character is limited to local environment; the quality of personality is universal in its influence, and originality is its fundamental element. All leaders, whether in politics or philosophy, art or literature, possess it, or they would not be leaders. The rare possessors of personality inspire four sentiments in the heart of man; namely, love, envy, respect, and hatred. Personality is inimitable, and yet it is mimicked more than anything else. A man's temperament is all the man. It is more than his style, because a gifted writer can vary his style, but his temperament never. Indeed, when Count Tolstoy changed his mode of living, when he set aside worldly pleasures, vices, and ambitions, he could not lay aside the domineering temperament with which he was born. Used to commanding people in his younger days, he expects to command still. This sort of man will never consent to learn from others; he would compel people to learn from him. And this is the danger. Men juggle with "temperament" as they do with words, phrases, theories, whims, and fads; and it rarely occurs to people who reason from a sentimental standpoint to analyze their feelings.

Stamp with a seal of sincerity any preposterous theory, and there will not be found wanting sentimental people to accept it. Nor can you ever convince the sentimental dreamer that sincerity is no more a mark of genius or wisdom, than writing a novel every year is a sign of talent. Self-confidence and the fanatical instinct develop and proceed apace; and what is this self-confidence but the most positive form of sincerity? Wise men not only make blunders, but often doubt their own powers. They have their negative moments. A fanatic never doubts. It is this perennial assurance which gives him such sway over the masses, and hypnotizes many intelligent people, so that they accept mere will for reason.

Tolstoy and Ibsen are two names which are frequently pronounced in the same breath, but it would be difficult to find two men more widely separated, both by temperament and by method. Tolstoy began life as an aristocratic *viveur*, changed his mode of living, and became a preacher with a system. Ibsen, on the contrary, presents ideas and images from the poetic side of life. He is no more a preacher than Shakespeare, yet the examples he sets before us have all the vividness and ardor of the real. Such work requires something besides power and sincerity; for we are here in the presence of the poetic instinct, which is not only a temperament, but a state of culture that is clairvoyant in its very nature.

This nature cannot be assumed at will, whereas the builder of systems may begin life as he pleases. There is no fixed time for him to appear on the program of life's races; and he may always count on winning at least one "popular" race. When a single idea takes possession of a man of talent to the exclusion of all others, his thought becomes entangled, his reason no longer holds the balance of power in favor of sound judgment and artistic imagination. One has only to look at the portrait of Count Tolstoy to see a man of iron will, possessed by a fixed idea. It is not a head we can compare with that of an Emerson or a Goethe. The face is characterized by an expression of distrust, suspicion, and dogged will- the antithesis of those signs which are characteristic of harmonious minds.

There has not been during the past century a more striking example of provincial ascendancy springing from dogmatic will. And yet the celebrated Russian is sincere. But his sincerity is born of a certain inherent, unconscious hauteur, which is the cause of so much oracular positiveness. Like Carlyle, he is positive from lack of experience. His reasons, too, are not the reasons of the poet, whose inspirations are both deep and lofty, subtle and lucid, but those of a writer looking at life on a surface without reflective lights. He takes long, solemn views of men and things, outlooks that correspond with the long, bleak, and lonely wastes of the Russian steppes. But the solemnity is that of the old-time preacher, at once strong and narrow, never broad and universally appropriate.

The abrupt is as dangerous in man as it is in Nature: there has been no graded development in the march of this singular character. The contrast between the fashionable, worldly Tolstoy and the Tolstoy suddenly become ethical gives the mind a shock. Harmonious thinkers are never precipitate. They move from one sphere to another with analytical caution and patient reserve. They are patient above all things, waiting years before accepting a new system where superficial minds wait months. The man who is swayed by emotion or passion is never certain in his judgment. And this uncertainty renders him a victim to appearance and illusion. Urged on by a powerful emotion, he jumps in the dark; his efforts appear successful, in reality they are failures. Tolstoy's efforts have made the wealthy realize more than ever the absurdity of the idea of universal equality and humility; because, having plenty of time to consider calmly the questions which the great writer sets before them, they not only refuse to leap in the dark, but they recognize the impossibility of his system being established successfully.

If the body cries out against pain, the mind grows violent in its revolt against pressure. This is the one insupportable thing for the spirit of man, the thing which is most antipathic to every fiber of his being. The idea that he is to obscure his identity by merging his temperament in that of a thousand or a million others is impossible for most minds to entertain seriously. Culture is mighty in a modest way. It rises above the fads and fashions of crowds, and remains fixed upon an adamantine basis for all time. This accounts for Greek immortality. This also accounts for the ephemeral character of Roman power. For the powerful must finally take its rank in the category of the evanescent and the material.

Culture is never loud or ambitious, but there is a fatal

something behind it which pushes it unconsciously into prominence. The most transcendent Greek minds moved in an atmosphere of seeming indifference, and it may be taken as a maxim that when a writer addresses himself to the multitude his influence will diminish and his followers dwindle with time. Power, in the worldly sense, is synonymous with decay. The deeds and influence of Alexander, Caesar, and Bonaparte were short-lived, but the aphorisms of Marcus Aurelius are as potent today as when they were written. Aurelius possessed the calm, inherent vitality of Grecian culture which made him insensible to the allurements of power. The meteors which cross our night path through space burst almost as soon as their light appears. And so with modern superstitions.

IMITATION AND ORIGINALITY

The assertion of John Stuart Mill that new melody will some day be impossible to invent seems true, for since Wagner we have had little save imitations of the oppressive and tedious side of his genius. But if this be true of music, art is in the same predicament. The world is passing from the purely artistic to the commonplace and pseudo-artistic. Artists are left with the alternative of returning to primitive methods or persisting in that kind of mechanical imitation so cunningly wrought by painters like Meissonier.

Does not this dilemma explain the abortive attempts of the French symbolists to imbue their angular, weirdly incoherent pictures with the semblance of life? Art-symbolism is not likely to produce such a master as Maeterlinck is in literature, for the reason that in poetic symbolism the mind is charmed and instructed by a different psychological process. The eye demands, above all things, the highest, simplest, and most natural expression of physical beauty. Symbolical artists, in despair of being original, have sought to adapt the metaphysical to the plastic by a mixture of medieval mysticism, spiritism, and the naive impotence of Botticelli. The result is a mystical incoherence, a straining after a form of originality that is neither realistic nor idealistic in its effect. The critical eye is more often offended than pleased with this new experiment in art. And, after all, are we not too human in these days for the worship of the attenuated and ethereal? Since asceticism is no longer considered a reasonable indulgence, the world has come to believe in the natural and the normal as the true mode of plastic inspiration.

The creative faculty, which means genius in poetry and music, is limited to such a degree in plastic art that many painters of renown are intellectually inferior to the mechanical dexterity of the hand, so to speak. Unlike the poet and the musician, they need the model. So nearly is their talent related to formula and method, that in many respects it resembles a science more than a gift. It is an art which acts on the emotions through optical sensation, and may be likened to the talent of the actor which depends on the dramatist for the development of character and on, the enthusiasm of local assemblies for inspiration.

Compare the work of the great masters with the best work of the new generation, and the sensation is like that experienced in passing from a garden of flowers to a field of red clover. The early masters especially had the secret possessed by the Athenian sculptors, which Joseph Roux defined in the aphorism: "The Greek statue blushed; the modern statue makes the beholder blush." What strikes the visitor on entering the celebrated galleries is the warmth of the coloring, the vivid and lifelike expression, the marvelous richness and eclat of the ensemble displayed in a Da Vinci, a Correggio, a Raphael, or a Titian, in contradistinction to the pictures of the modern schools. The visitor is drawn to the works of the old masters by something which is not only poetic, but real; there is a magnetic warmth and mellowness about the tone and expression of their portraits which attracts as by a perpetual charm.

The enormous success of Meissonier's pictures is the surest sign that our taste in art has degenerated. A Parisian critic has defined his work as the "triumph of the bourgeois instinct in art"; and in this connection it is interesting to note the remarkable harmony existing between many writers and artists of the day. There is a striking affinity between the methods of Meissonier and the manner of Zola. Both have depicted life with power and precision; both have painted in colors or in words the form of thought most congenial to their minds. But their creative faculties end precisely in the element in which they were developed. They are masters of the powerful, students of the Darwinian theory applied to materialistic art. Meissonier has glorified the most extravagant period in the military history of

France. In his vivid illustrations of events in the career of Bonaparte the painter has only expressed his personal predilection for the most ambitious of modern generals; that is to say, he has given vent to a sentiment in favor of a survival of the fittest in the matter of brute force and inexorable egoism. A painter depicts with the brush the things that are most congenial to his sentiment. He can no more rise above his natural disposition than a poet can rise beyond the limits of his poetic faculty. In his figures of Bonaparte, Meissonier sought to turn an idol of flesh and blood into a personage of transcendent heroism; in his figures of Christ, Munkacsy has debased the ideal man to the attitude of a half-starved madman. Realism has bent its forces towards the expression of an art that lies beyond the creative ability of its votaries. The charm of beauty is replaced by efforts which show restrictions of taste and weakness of judgment. The same physiological traits, the same corporeal preponderance that stamps contemporary art in general, characterize the work of Munkacsy.

In his *Portraitures of Christ* he shows us not the "divine idea" in the man, but the figure of a Nihilistic fanatic, who, from the wild expression in his face and undignified attitude of his person, causes the beholder little surprise to find that he stands before Pilate as a dangerous disturber of the peace. The people who surround Christ are a little more modern than the Hungarian gypsy and a little more Oriental than the Hungarian Jew.

We are living in an age when technical skill is supposed to be as good as imagination in art. The accuracy with which a Meissonier or a Degas paints a battle or a ballet-dancer is equaled by the photographic word-pictures drawn by a Maupassant or a Zola. Take, for example, *Notre Coeur.* With what power the different scenes are depicted; with what accuracy every phrase sets before the eye a living, moving personage; with what realistic art the temperament of each is made to unroll before the reader as by a word-panorama, where every page tells precisely what it ought to tell, and where every scene contains exactly what was intended. The author, striving after originality, has done his utmost to go beyond the commonplace; but one puts down the book with the feeling that Maupassant, although a master of the technical part of story-telling, lacked the faculty of poetic invention. His heroes and heroines are photographs of individuals who swarm in the fashionable world of Paris, and who, far from representing rare types of humanity, only appear on paper the common symbol of latter-day society as it exists in all the great cosmopolitan centers of the world.

The critical reader is interested in this kind of work from the assurance that the characters and incidents shall unroll before him in due order from the first to the last line of the book. As for the characters, the reader is held by that kind of interest which attaches to the secret springs of a mechanical mermaid, or the platitudes of a modern *Parisienne*. Maupassant puts his characters through a course of literary gymnastics, in which he shows us the muscles, the sinews, the *esprit*, the mental maneuvers of each; and when the entertainment is over we realize its artificial methods, and wonder at the author's power to hold the reader's attention by such trivial devices.

There never was a time when so much art was wasted on subjects and plots which in themselves are ephemeral. Guy de Maupassant was a pupil of Gustave Flaubert, and he did his utmost to reach the artistic height of his master. But it is impossible, after having read *La Tentation de Saint-Antoine* or Madame Bovary not to notice the wide gap that separates the two authors: Flaubert was intuitive, creative, lucid in his artistic conceptions, without a flaw in the arrangement of his ideas; Maupassant shows all those signs of technical subtlety and perfect literary form which were characteristic of his master, but the indefinable tone of sincerity and poetic power possessed by the author of *Salammbo* is lacking. It is the difference between talent carried to a state of perfection by sheer application, and genius which is born with the creative and poetic instinct. Take from a novel like *Notre Coeur*, its rhetorical perfection, and the story itself would be insupportable. Such works are not merely imitative, they revolve in a social sphere that borders on the inhuman: wives without the maternal instinct, friends without affection, lovers without love, honor without conscience, everything that paints the modern *canaille* and the social *sans culotte* of the fashionable world of today.

We are told that reality in the unreal is the truest form of art, and to photograph the emptiest phase of modern art is put down as the quintessence of artistic ability. Balzac imitated, but he added to the faculty of imitation a philosophic and poetic conception that gave to his work an originality which places it beside the most original in literature. Zola, an admirer and follower of Balzac, has not succeeded in reaching the plane of his great predecessor any more than Maupassant attained the perfection of Flaubert. We have arrived at a time when novelists have taken to the model, when those who seem the strongest cannot walk without the support of some "school" or method, whereby the machinery of the intellect may be regulated and set in motion.

The longer we contemplate the work already done, the more the world of art and literature appears to be in repose on the pillars of that work; and the time is at hand for a true realization of the facts as they exist.

Nevertheless, the man of talent or genius today has a sphere of his own, which, if not creative in the sense of former times, is even more difficult when we consider the vast observation, experience, and general knowledge required to impress serious minds. Three centuries ago Bacon, while yet a young man, did not hesitate to declare that he had taken "all knowledge unto his province." But at that day there was little to master beyond the classical confines of the Greek and Latin world. Both style and model were invariably borrowed from the ancients; no weight was attached to the methods and manners of medieval thought. Bacon, therefore, in taking all knowledge unto his province simply appropriated the intellectual possessions of Greece and Rome, and out of them formulated a new system of reasoning.

Emerson was wrong when he said that a man could learn as much by staying at home as by going abroad. The man who expects to rise above mediocrity in this age must not only become familiar with the characteristics of his own people, but must acquaint himself with the virtues and vanities of other nations in order to wear off the provincial veneer which adheres to all individuals without practical experience, and mocks one in a too conscious security of contentment or indifference. Talent was never so rife as at present; what is rare is a universality of thought and feeling, a union of the intuitional and experimental, a clear connection between knowledge and wisdom- application on the one hand, comprehension on the other. It no longer suffices to familiarize oneself with the dead languages and the philosophy of the ancients, for a new criterion has been established whereby to judge the man of creative ability.

The genius of the future must be acquainted with the world, not only in its poetic but its prosaic attire. He must be familiar with the mystic elements of Athenian philosophy and the characteristics of German pessimism, modern evolution, scientific agnosticism; sentiment must be coupled with science, and philosophy with art. The ideas and formulae of one mind no longer suffice to wield an absolute power in the world of thought; the best intellects of all ages must be assimilated and appropriated in order to bring forth new manifestations of the creative faculty which shall add something more to the wisdom already expressed by that indefinable quality we designate as genius.

PHYSICAL COURAGE AND MORAL COWARDICE

Physical courage and moral cowardice are usually found as twins. When France was "la grande nation militaire" no one dared to speak his mind. The chief quality of the nation resided in physical valor, which was supposed to embody all the moral virtues.

But with Louis XVI military force took a second rank; men began to preach what they thought. France has ever since remained the only country where literary and philosophical truths have been enunciated without fear or favor by individuals as well as by groups and schools. On the other hand, Spain has remained a physical-force nation, as is shown by her bull-rings. The bull-fighters face death voluntarily every day; and yet the Spaniards remain as putty in the hands of the priests. England, since the days of Elizabeth, has not only been the leading naval Power, but she has added a number of more or less brutal sports to the list of valorous pastimes: foot-ball, fox-hunting, prize-fighting, require plenty of muscle and physical courage, but no brains or moral independence. It is considered "highly respectable" to be a soldier, or a sailor, or an athlete, or a fox-hunter, without sufficient intelligence to engage in the most superficial conversation on art, music, or literature. It is considered risky to speak of religious doubt, although you may be an Agnostic; bad taste not to admire cricket-playing, although it may bore you.

It is difficult to be a race of athletes and progress artistically and socially at the same time. This physical courage and commercial activity develop a certain hypocrisy in the English character. Frankness, generosity, enthusiasm are rarely expressed with a free hand in regard to meritorious works in literature, poetry, philosophy, and art. Many writers are slow to praise, fearing that frank enthusiasm will be taken as a mark of critical incapacity; so hypocrisy bows, and gives a blow for each word of praise uttered. Another form of dissimulation is that of beginning a criticism by the hypercritical method, and ending it by eulogy. Before any praise is rendered the author or artist receives a certain number of stripes with a literary cat-o'nine-tails, and this passes for criticism in certain quarters.

In literature the English are a sentimental people; and it is a fine art with the critic to devise means to make the reader suppose the critic superior to that kind of thing. The result is that the people go their own way, and read the books that please them, without a thought for the critic's opinion. No one who has watched the effect produced by certain popular authors can doubt this. Many authors, however, who are not popular, intimidated by the system of scourging, have been turned into literary tortoises, not daring to show more than a nose now and again of their real self. This is why English literature of the present day is so devoid of color and personality. The lack of sincerity engenders hypercriticism. One wonders how writers can find the courage, not to say patience, to go on from day to day concocting articles in which none but provincial minds believe and none but the idle read. An excuse is made for praising anything good, whether in art or literature, especially if the work shows personality, for that is what the worshipers of physical courage hate more than anything else; and so it is in all branches of art and thought; new forms, aspirations, achievements must be received with caution, if not with suspicion. There is one thing, however, which the physical courage people accept, namely, humor. This accounted for the great success of the new Scotch humor. No meditation was required in reading it, and every one could appreciate it, from butlers to bishops, especially when it was not only orthodox but sentimental.

One of the most curious effects of moral cowardice on the British mind is shown in the attitude of the majority of the leading writers of the day towards questions such as Socialism,

Spiritism, Skepticism, etc. Hundreds who sympathize with Socialism, or believe in Spiritism, hide their convictions behind a mask of irony or humor. British humor, in these days, is not so much a natural product of the mind and heart, as a cloak to dissemble thought. Anything will pass if dressed up in that humoristic garb which harmonizes with those "manly sports" we are taught to believe as so essential to the glory of Englishmen, because humor is one of the prime elements in these sports, it being an element which springs from the tongue, wholly foreign to reason and thought. And this is why physical courage, carried to excess, always leads to moral skulking. It is a curious fact that of all the great nations none do so little thinking as the English and the Spanish, the two nations that deal most in sports. An Englishman of the lower order is troubled by nothing if he can get plenty of beer and tobacco, with plenty of rough amusement, just as the Spaniard thinks of nothing but attending mass and bull-fights.

When Matthew Arnold went to America, he said the curse of that country was its "funny men." To the English critic the journalists seemed to take nothing seriously, not even the critic, whom they included in their humoristic assaults. But American humor is as far removed from the English character, as French wit is from Teutonic sentiment. American humor is the result of intelligence directed in a single channel; English humor is meant to fill a gap left by moral apathy and mental indifference. The English say amusing things to a lazy and hypocritical public.

Put a French and an English mechanic face to face in an argument on politics or religion, and note the difference between the logic and frankness of the first and the obtuse subterfuges of the second. The French workman not only thinks, but is not afraid to say what he does think; his English brother lets sentiment fill the place of thought, and is always the victim of sentimental wire-pullers.

MODERN MYSTICISM

The new-woman movement, the Socialist movement, the Buddhist craze, and the psychical research movement, are all so many forces which Nature has put into the minds of certain men and women to react against the prevailing moral decadence. An Englishwoman in bloomer costume on a bicycle is a furious protest against an intolerable form of British prudery.

PARSIFALITIS

It was Schopenhauer who opened the eyes of the Germans to the futility of their dream-philosophers. With that writer the occupation of German visionaries came to an end, after which there was clearly nothing to be done but descend from the clouds and deal with first principles, with man in particular and humanity in general. But as the last philosophical dreamer disappeared, a genius arose with a new gift and a new ambition. Wagner, influenced by the example of Schopenhauer, became a musical metaphysician, who united something of Teutonic dream-life with the most positive form of art ever invented by man.

The climax of the new art-philosophy was reached in the mighty inspirations of *Der Ring des Nibelungen*, clearly conceived and powerfully embodied from the first line of the drama to the last detail of the *mise-en-scene*. Then came the Wagnerian decadence, and *Parsifal* was written. All previous systems were to be ignored for a method whereby a group of notes should possess the quality of asserting an individuality in an idea called the *leit-motif*. The music of the leading characters in the drama was to preach a kind of sermon to the emotions, and by constant iteration act as a spiritual interpreter to the understanding. The composer was to choose a motif much as a preacher would choose a text, and, at given moments throughout the work, reiterate the motif by different instruments and voices, just as the preacher might repeat his text with renewed emphasis several times during an exhortation. But just in proportion as a sermon is enhanced by the repetition of a text, so a musical ensemble is weakened by the iteration of a motif, especially when the impression created on a mind wholly free from bias is one of mediocrity.

Of all things, music should never pose, should never

bewilder the senses by meanings and motives hidden under a veil of theoretical uncertainty. The greater part of the music of Parsifal belongs to the domain of psychological experiment. And as it is impossible for obscure thought to take a plastic and external configuration, so it is impossible to produce a regular and artistic form by the methods employed by the master in this work.

In Parsifal, Wagner attempted to depict sentiments and emotions, as they come and go, with the rapidity of thought. In the short space of a few seconds he tries to express in music precisely what is supposed to pass in the mind of Parsifal or Kundry. Love, passion, frenzy, hope, malice, despair, he attempts to transfix by orchestral means, each chord varying in a multitudinous flow of sound, seldom halting long enough on any one idea for the listener to fix a definite form in his mind. All this is highly instructive from a psychological point of view; it is interesting as a metaphysical study, but it is not inspiration. Musical form demands precisely what is demanded of poetry and sculpture- repose, beauty, regularity, a satisfying sense of well rounded harmonies. While music finds a congenial element in mystical sentiment, in soft and violent emotions, in mental and religious passion, in pastoral and philosophical meditation, in joy and depression, it offers no envelope for recondite thought.

A musical mood, to be effective, must be prolonged to a certain degree. There is something in the nature of music which abhors jumps and vague transitions. In Parsifal the score is violent and abrupt when it is not languid and torpid. Its chief characteristics are a solemn listlessness on the one hand, and vague precipitation on the other. In the first part it is too positive, in the last part too negative. It begins by assertion and ends by renunciation. The effect of its teaching is not ascendancy, but mental and physical decadence. Strange perverseness of human nature that should lead two men so unlike each other- Tolstoy the Russian, and Wagner the German- to the same decadent proclivities, the first by literature and personal example, the second by literature and music. After the pleasures and triumphs of youth and middle age, the first ends by mending boots as an act of grace, the second by mending souls as an act of glory.

But this is not all. In Parsifal art has suffered. In Tannhauser and Lohengrin we have romance, sentiment, passion, a free and positive inspiration, and notwithstanding a vein of intense pessimistic melancholy running through them, they remain as monuments of inspirational achievement. But in Parsifal Wagner descended at one stroke to sentimentality pure and simple. The thinking world is asked to accept this work as a definite ethical pronouncement. We are expected to become so unphilosophical, so impractical, as to exchange our individuality for self-effacement and dumb resignation: an attitude that failed even in the incomparable presentation of Greek and Roman stoics; an attitude that so nullified the Hindu mind that India lost its self-control and finally its independence; an attitude that has reduced Italy, Austria, and Spain to a condition of vassalage, and has forced the Christian world to accept modern progress as a prop and modern science as an aid. Both the music and the drama of Wagner's last work tend to a climax of negative emotion, all the more dangerous because the work was conceived and written as an example of ethical art not to be surpassed even by the author himself. The active genius invariably ends by doing too much. It was so with Napoleon when he started for Moscow. The danger lies in excessive ambition, in the forcing of ideas when Nature calls for passive repose.

But not only does the active genius end by doing too much, with a temperament like that of Wagner he lands his followers on the wrong side of the ditch; he passes away in a cloud of glory, imposing on his disciples- who mistake mere ambition for inspiration a state of continual squabbling and contention. A militant genius, if he live long enough, ends by counteracting the effect of his most virile powers. Beethoven, whose temperament was meditative, had no systems to build and no theories to uphold. This is why in his works we find more order and logic in ideas, and more art and consonance in method. He was positive as a personality, but passive as an artist. Verdi, at his worst, is tolerable; Beethoven, at his worst, is interesting; Wagner, at his worst, is insupportable. The mission of music is to elevate and console, but there is a wide gulf between consolation and renunciation. Music should vivify, encourage, inspire, and comfort. A funeral march depresses the mind and degrades music. The reason is obvious- there is no consolation in a funeral march.

The melancholy in Wagner is so intense and poignant, that it often passes the poetic limit and becomes distressful. A sadness which surpasses the power of speech is the dominant note of Lohengrin, Tannhauser, and the Flying Dutchman. And be it said- with profound admiration and respect- after listening to these great works we do not carry away with us a feeling of relief and encouragement, but one of singular and indefinable depression. In the Master's company we are carried to the heavens, as in the Ride of the Valkyries, or lowered to the depths, as in the overture to the Flying Dutchman. And if we feel electrified by his flights, we are fascinated by the breadth and depth of his labyrinthine pessimism. The art, the science, and the passion of his melancholy have never been equaled; but it is the passion and the poetry of twilight without the hope of dawn. Wagner is Schopenhauer set to music.

In the psychological world there are a thousand different diseases which attack the mind; here it is religion, there it is philosophy, science, or art. Credulity on the one hand, or positivism on the other, are symptoms of psychological distemper. Those who deny genius are affected as well as those who blindly accept the nonsense that genius sometimes preaches. Perhaps Democritus who laughs is as mentally afflicted as

Heraclitus who weeps; and Diogenes, who lived in a tub, was no worse or better off than Alexander who slept on the sands of the Persian desert. Nature, smiling blandly at all, has her own secret, which is eternally hidden.

Parsifalitis is a new distemper in the world of art. It attacks man at two of his most vulnerable points, his imagination and his instinct of credulity. It entraps by the splendor of its mise-en-scene, by its metaphysics, and by the hallucinating movements of gesture and sound. In the auditorium at Bayreuth, where optical and acoustic conditions are perfect, where a thousand persons gaze at the same sights, listen to the same sounds, think of the same things, the general effect is intensely hypnotic. It is not strange that under such conditions, romantic, neurotic, and sentimental minds should be acted upon by a force far beyond their will to withstand. Here the fanatically disposed settle themselves for an abracadabrant initiation into the mysteries of the Parsifalian chimera. Each time the curtains are parted a new door opens on a world of illusive suggestion; at the end of each act one more door closes upon the personal judgment of the listener. The typical habitues of Bayreuth, tormented by a fixed idea, their nerves shattered by the abuse of antithetical harmonies, advise the new-comer to have patience. "After the fifteenth representation of Parsifal you will begin to appreciate the beauty of the score and the sense of the symbols." The visitor promises to return again, and half through snobbery, half through curiosity, he becomes inoculated with the germs of Parsifalitis without once suspecting the danger. Then comes a time when the world of art has no longer anything beautiful or instructive to offer.

Bayreuth has shorn the "constant visitor" of his personality, of his judgment, of his appreciation of the artistic and the beautiful. A monk, confined in the cell of a somber monastery, enjoys more intellectual freedom; he rejoices in the works of a hundred different saints; he is free to admire a certain priest more than a certain bishop, a certain bishop more than a certain pope. The victim of Parsifalitis knows but one priest, who is at once both pope and saint, the high-priest of the Grail. An acolyte of the temple of Bayreuth is sworn to a kind of secret compact to burn incense only at one altar of this temple, in the chapel of Parsifal, and nowhere else. But if Parsifal causes an obsession at Bayreuth, on British soil it has produced a new form of snobbery. In this country snobbery favors the most successful master, whoever he may be. The snob waits until the early disciples of genius have done the rough and needy work, plowed the ground, planted the seed, and reaped the harvest; he then appears at the vintage festival with all the assurance and satisfaction of the successful reaper.

In Thackeray's day the snob was almost exclusively confined to social circles. From the social sphere he invaded that of art. The studios and the galleries became thronged at certain seasons with people devoid of the sense of color and unconscious of the beauty of form. But the British snob, always behind the snob of other nations in his intellectual manifestations, makes up for lost time when he once decides upon a move; so, from art he has jumped to ultra-Wagnerian music. Conceive, if you can, a sudden change in literary taste from Shakespeare to Mr. Gilbert, or from Mr. Gilbert to Ibsen, and you will appreciate the chasm that has been crossed at a single bound by the latest and most pretentious form of snobbery. It is an easy matter to affect admiration for painters and composers, but difficult to simulate it for poets and philosophers; mere sentiment suffices for the former, but the latter demand ideas. This is another reason why artistic snobbery commonly moves on well-beaten ground. Exclamations and platitudes will do to hide one's ignorance of art and music; but you cannot juggle with the productions of an Ibsen, a Meredith, or a Maeterlinck. Is this not why the new snobbery, in its jump from art to music, has leaped over literature without so much as touching a poet or philosopher in its passage? For it is an error to suppose that the admiration kindled by writers like Schopenhauer and Nietzsche is tinctured with snobbery. The snob, no matter what his learning may be, will never patronize anything which requires serious justification by word or pen.

45

AUTHORITY AND INDIVIDUALISM

When one takes the stand of an independent onlooker, freed from the prejudices of creeds and systems, events which seem to the short-sighted mere accidents appear as grave and solemn occurrences in the march of destiny. Great changes in the political and social world are not caused by caprice, but by the gradual death of tradition. This gives place to a new form of thought one degree in advance of the old.

When Louis XVI lost his head, monarchy in France was doomed. That event, which the superficial regarded as a mere accident, served as a warning and a prophecy to the wise, and through it not a few thinkers regarded the downfall of Charles X and of Louis Philippe as inevitable. The wheel of events is never reversed. All governments, systems, sects, come to an end and give place to new ones. But nothing vanishes suddenly. Systems, like men, wear themselves out, not by sudden friction, nor by fits and starts, but by stages as definitely marked on the map of time as the stages of a desert route for the marching of caravans.

In the movements of certain Eastern dances the contortions of the performers seem out of harmony with the rhythm of the music; nevertheless the character of the people, the music, and the gestures are one; the jerky and the seemingly accidental are but the natural changes from one mood to another, symphonic gradations in a series of scenes developed in accordance with the tastes and the temperaments of different tribes and peoples. In politics, philosophy, religion, the transitions may also seem sudden and meaningless; but the illusions of sight and sentiment are chimerical symbols which often haunt the mind and heart of the most robust at a time when reason and clear sight are the most necessary. In the movement of great bodies there are incidents, but no accidents; issues and results, but no haphazard upheavals and endings. There would

have been no war for American Independence without
Puritanism, no war for the freeing of the slaves without
Republicanism, no Salvation Army without Wesleyanism. Look
where we may, this law of progression has ruled from the
beginning. When Garibaldi entered Rome at the head of an army
the temporal power of the Pope was at an end, after which the
proclamation of papal infallibility was a mere announcement
without political or practical meaning. In whatsoever sphere of
action we may look, the bare menace of authority is sufficient to
designate the trend of developing opinions. As thought precedes
words, so words develop into actions: deeds are the direct result
of opinions; and opinions, in our day, point to the destruction of
isolated authority and the leveling of distinctive qualities into
utilitarianism.

The psychological influences at work, secretly and
silently, moving slowly on in a determined direction, like the
slow rising of waters in a plain when the sun steadily melts the
snows of uninhabitable heights, impress the mind of the thinker
with wonder and awe. And what a study for the thinker! We have
witnessed not only the decadence, but the death of individual
authority. Modem hero worship began with Bonaparte and ended
with Carlyle. The Corsican made it familiar, the Scottish moralist
made it fashionable. Democracy rendered it impossible. Nor
does history record an instance of a nation having been saved
from impending disaster by a prophet. Lord Chesterfield
predicted the French Revolution thirty years before the event;
Chateaubriand foretold the advent of French Republicanism
nearly half a century previous to the tragedy at Sedan; and
Moltke, with a cynicism which some writers regard as a species
of sorcery, devised and concocted a system of operations for the
taking of Paris and the overthrow of the Empire as early as
1857, thirteen years before the declaration of war, at a time when
the Palace of the Tuileries was the universal rendezvous of kings,
millionaires, and beautiful women, in the midst of one of the
most luxurious, peaceful, and promising reigns of modern

history.

The fact that a man exists who can see a generation or two in advance is in itself a symbol of fatality. A prophet is synonymous with destiny. He is among us not as an example, but as a symbol; not as a warning, but as a figure. The true prophet, while preaching to this world, lives in another far remote. He is the shadow of the unknown; and shadows may frighten for a moment, but they do not impress. What passes as a flash is not understood by men devoid of intuitive insight; for as it requires the highest culture to recognize the early manifestations of genius, it requires something akin to the prophetic spirit to recognize a prophet. The recognition of prophetic truth cannot be imparted, and for this reason the people who follow genius at the outset are destined to be so few in number as to be devoid of worldly power. And so, in spite of everything, a prophet is synonymous with destiny. This is why the lamentations of Jeremiah and Isaiah, even now, make the most curious and the most melancholy as well as the most fascinating reading. Their powerful inspirational outbursts did not save Israel, not even at a time when a prophet was regarded as a mouthpiece of Jehovah.

In the Anglo-Saxon nations the signs of coming events may be likened to those of France in the latter half of the eighteenth century when that country lost, in rapid succession, Canada, India, and her possessions in Africa, when the caustic negations of Voltaire met half-way the imbecile quarrels of the Jansenists, who, blind to the universal disaster and decadence, found time for violent disputes about the doctrine of predestination, thus assisting by intestine discord the rush towards the brink of national calamity and social chaos. In every case we find political disaster stalking arm-in-arm with religious dissension. There are three principal social elements which are leveling and diluting old systems and beliefs- the Salvation Army, which has made a clean divorce between Episcopalianism and the people; Republicanism, which has undermined Monarchism; and Socialism, which has denied even the necessity of Republicanism. The Roman Republic passed upward into the splendors of the Empire.

The duration of its decline seemed destined to correspond with the height of its glory by a long series of tragic disasters. But in our day society is not imitating the Romans. Socialism, if it is to come, will not mount towards Empire; it seeks a rapid descent to a level of individual equality. If the idealism with which we are familiar is spiritual and intuitive, the science of the near future will be founded on commonsense and individual needs, without which idealism itself is but a sounding brass and a tinkling cymbal. Intelligence in the past was almost always turned to personal authority instead of to philosophical influence and example. Indeed, authority seems to have been the chief aim in the lives of most men who have acted on the stage of public affairs, whether in politics, in religion, or in art. And the liberty which authoritative people give themselves even now is often worse than the license they profess to cure. Nor is the individualism here displayed of the kind which is intended to work both ways; it works but one way, and that on the side of egoism; for when it comes to liberty of conscience and utterance, the vaunted freedom is found wanting- it is vested in one man or a single group of men.

The evolution of one law is in harmony with the progress of all other laws. In the secret methods of the unseen there is a fixed mode of progression based on social and antithetic harmony. People allude to the new-woman movement, to socialistic plans and progress as fashionable and evanescent fads. Few there are who can see the graded descent in government, the transitions in creeds, the merging of the classes into the masses, the aristocratic into the democratic. The secret forces of Nature, commonly dual in their action, are now opposing optimistic science to pessimistic religion, mystical idealism to agnostic uncertainty. But a nation which advances towards the declivity which precedes decay is harassed by a thousand inimical forms of thought, which seem to rise from regions previously ignored or unknown. It is a hidden and unrecognized law that the first signs of national decadence are marked by indifference and egoism on one hand, and loud professions of optimism on the other; for one-half of the community is blinded by obtuseness and apathy, the other by avidity and imprudence, as if an evil enchantress had nullified, as with a magic wand, the judgment of the rulers and the understanding of the people.

The world is, therefore, likely to have a manifestation of anarchic collectivism before it can reach the natural and congenial element of individual liberty, when men can move about in perfect harmony with their fellows and yet retain distinctive traits of character and genius. Society will probably be composed of small groups working in harmony with one another. Universal agreement may be attained, but universal affinity never. The chemical constituents of each separate human entity forbid an affinity where large numbers of people are massed together under a regime of collective authority. Individual freedom will come about after freedom has been attained, first politically, then religiously, then philosophically; for this is the order in which Nature began her social development. Therefore we have had, and are still having, political agitations always closely identified with religious liberty, tyranny, and inharmony, the question of individual liberty coming in only by vague suggestion and isolated example. Socialism will strip society of its false aristocracy. Socialism, in its turn, will be conquered and governed by the aristocracy of intellect, the only unconquerable thing in the world.

THE NEW CRITICISM

It would be interesting to ask certain critics to define the difference between the personal merits of a poet who has periods of alcoholic inebriation, and a poet who has spells of narcotic intoxication. The people who idolize Burns and sneer at Poe, who hold Coleridge up as a philosophical paragon and frown at De Quincey as a literary outcast, may or may not know that petty, local, or provincial prejudice is at the bottom of their likes and dislikes. The calm observer, the man who takes the world as it is, the impartial judge, knows now, as he ever has known, that this kind of criticism is not worth the weight of a pinch of snuff in the critical balance which holds the burden of genius. When we stop to consider the small number of criticisms which are not based on this kind of provincial sentiment, as offensive in its ignorance as it is monstrous in its impertinence, we cannot wonder that genius in the Anglo-Saxon nations means the battle of a lifetime.

We cannot marvel that it took twenty years for Ruskin to convince the people that Turner was the greatest of our painters, and forty years for George Meredith to climb the rugged hill of fame. Even in these days of supposed culture, criticism, in many places, means the liberty to render sentimental preferences conspicuous by the prejudice displayed in sustaining them. The partiality of the sentimental critics is so apparent, that it is no wonder they do more harm than good to the genius whom they seek to uphold. We regard with stupefaction today the adverse opinions expressed by Carlyle about certain poets and writers of his time. Our sense of justice, our experience, our knowledge of the world, our international sympathies, cause us to look upon such criticism as the product of a narrow and prejudiced age. All criticism uttered in passion or prejudice dies with the man who utters it. In Carlyle's day a false sentiment set up an authority founded on inexperience and self-assurance.

MODERN MYSTICISM

A pseudo- intuition gave certain writers the semblance of oracles. That philosopher was supposed to receive all callers, and between a puff of his pipe and a cup of tea he would answer a vital question by an epithet that was certain to prejudice the visitor against some new manifestation of genius; the visitor, in his turn, would go forth and publish to the world the calumnious gossip as the solemn expression of a recognized prophet. Today we no longer accept an opinion if it be not sustained by actual experience, intimate knowledge, and a broad intellectual and social sympathy. We have become as skeptical and suspicious in literature as the modern chemist is in science. We no longer put faith in the opinions of a writer who knows but one country, one literature, one religion, and one philosophy. We wish to know what a critic has seen and heard, with what amount of culture he was born, and what he has attained by travel and hard fact. The judgment of a writer who criticizes a people with whom he has not had familiar intercourse can no longer be taken seriously. The influence of the old-fashioned intuitive critic was two-fold: he was accepted by the superstitious as a mouthpiece of divinity, and by the sentimental as a kind of demi-god supposed to possess the clairvoyant power of judging a man without having seen him, and of criticizing his works without having read them. Between superstition and sensibility there was no antagonism. It was considered the proper thing for the literary high-priest to pronounce; the intuitive oracle commanded with all the aplomb of a Spanish revolutionist issuing a manifesto. His chief characteristic was to believe his opinion infallible. There could be but one school, one sentiment, one religion, one literature; the critic was never a man who could learn by studying other writers, other nations. Or, if he turned his attention to a foreign author, it was to the exclusion of others of the same nationality, or of those of a rival nation.

If the Germans were praised, the French were ignored; if the French were found interesting, the Germans were declared stupid. The critic was always on the scent for authors whose work appeared to support, even in the vaguest way, his fads and his *isms*. When we look back at the criticism of fifty or even twenty years ago, we wonder at the number of authors who had the courage to think for themselves.

It seems but yesterday that Matthew Arnold was considered too advanced as a critic; at present much of his thought strikes us as tainted with provincialism. How far away the men and the isms of 1875 appear! And how vain does all past criticism seem! There is a growing sentiment that even Ruskin is fallible. He who was considered so cultured and so catholic is beginning to appear narrow and prejudiced. Sainte-Beuve lived long enough to be ignored by a whole school of writers. Old houses and churches may be renovated, but the mind of a critic grown moldy with systems never can be. Such is the stubbornness of human ambition that neither glory nor poverty, nor fatigue nor mental decay will restrain it. But one cannot help wondering at the conceit which permits educated men to expect the world to accept and abide by their maxims from one generation to another, as if all other mortals had nothing to do but be led by the nose, yea, and be made to swallow the nostrums of the sexagenarian while the nose is held.

A wise critic of fifty or sixty should renew his mind by meeting the latest phases of talent at the starting-point, saluting original and budding genius, seeking to understand the new temperaments, and, instead of letting the new-comers overtake and pass him, move on in harmony with them. By this means the critic would remain perennially in touch with every phase of thought worthy of the name. A young critic has an advantage over the old ones- he appropriates the wisdom of his elders, and profits by the sympathy, example, and inspiration of his confreres. But the inevitable reaction has come.

The persiflage, doubt, suspicion, skepticism, the supercilious sneer, have passed, as by a process of magic, from the tripod of antiquated authority to the crucible of the modern analyst, in which the opinions, theories, systems, and ethics of thirty years ago are differentiated in so impartial a fashion as to leave but a "trace" of those critical elements once considered so vital.

The young critic has learned to think for himself. He has put aside the idea of hero-worship as demoralizing and superannuated. Have not common-sense and a feeling of universal confraternity taught him that all men and women are heroic who have worked, waited, and suffered without losing faith in themselves? He knows, too, that there are scores of such people in cities like London and Paris. He feels that to put forward one man as a demi-god because fortuitous circumstances and a long life have made him famous, to select one poet to shine above all others, is carrying sentimental favoritism to an absurd, unjust, and painful degree. The optimism of the critic of yesterday was not always sound. He had a penchant for preaching, but his sermons were usually the outcome of pet illusions which grew in proportion with the number of his followers Seeing his off-hand opinions accepted as scientific facts, he became bolder every year, until at last he wielded a scepter mightier than that of most kings.

The critics of fifty years ago were sentimental pessimists disguised as optimists; the new critic is a sentimental skeptic. He is a poet who loves science, a dreamer who is not visionary, a philosopher who rejects systems, a conscious victim of sentimental atavism, a Democritus disposed to laugh in order to keep from weeping, a thinker who wishes to see the world as it is instead of as it is thought to be by mentors who sit at home and issue critical mandates respecting people and things they have never seen. It is not wholly by experience that the new critic is skeptical; he was born a doubter. The old critic believed in many things for which there was no proof; the new one believes little of what he sees and less of what he hears. But in

his skepticism there is a sympathetic element which was wholly
lacking in the haughty attitude of his predecessors. He doubts not
only others, but himself, and this not from affectation or choice,
but from compulsion; for he is conscious of the universal
fallibility of the human mind, especially of the mind of the critic.

MODERN MYSTICISM

AMIEL

Cast your line into the troubled waters of the moralist, sound his heart, dive still further, clutching at the craggy projections in the descent of his metaphysics, harpoon the monster in the obscurity of his thought, and you will have caught- what? a balloon of air, which cannot rise to the empyrean of free thought owing to an overload of ballast. To follow him do not seek to mount with Pegasus- it takes a plummet to find the depth of a foundered vessel. The typical moralist is there, and nowhere else.

How curious is the study of their jargon of perfectibility! Go to the center of their *moi*, and you will arrive at a chaos of contradictions which shock reason and dissipate sympathy. Their presence among men makes one think of haunted houses which have become uninhabitable. Who could have lived with a Pascal or an Amiel? They tremble themselves and make others tremble. They impress one less as human entities than as spiritual beings whose movements and gestures startle and bewilder. They are, in certain respects, unapproachable; they are much more inaccessible than a Poe or a De Quincey, for we know their faults, and in spite of them these writers are accessible. With their vast and powerful imagination they possess so large an amount of human sympathy and sociability, that one does not think of their weaknesses. The writers who repel are those who fear themselves and inspire fear in others.

Take, for example, Amiel, Scherer, and Naville. They were moralists of the old school, of the same country, and friends withal. Yet each found the metaphysics of the others insupportable. Amiel says: "Scherer etait l'intelligence de la conscience, Naville la moralite de la conscience, et moi la conscience de la conscience; un terrain commun, mais des individualites diverses"- "Scherer was the intelligence of conscience, Naville the morality of conscience, and I the conscience of conscience; a common ground but diverse individualities." Precisely. And this ground is the tenebrous bed of the ocean of metaphysics. "J'ai horreur d'etre dupe," he says, "done l'humiliation est le chagrin que je redoute encore le plus, et par consequent l'orgueil serait le plus profond de mes vices."- "I have a horror of being duped, hence, humiliation is the chagrin which I fear still more, and, in consequence, pride must be my greatest weakness." Pride, whose twin-sister is fear, is the inveterate evil of the moralists. Each says to himself: "I fear falling into the abyss like yourself, but my self-esteem is still stronger than my fear, consequently I cannot accept your system of morals; on the contrary, permit me to teach you my system, the only true one."

After having read thirty pages of Amiel one feels that one understands the secret of his weakness. A dreamer, who continually revolves in the same orbit, he possesses more sentiment than emotion, more sensations than ideas. It is experience that he lacks. Instead of traveling, he lost five years among the philosophical dreamers of Berlin- he who already was too much given to dreaming for Germany from 1843 to 1848 was a country of dreamers nourished on metaphysical diet.

In reading Amiel one receives the impression of a thinker who has lived at an epoch completely removed from ours. Much of what he says might have been said by some mystic of a past century; and the truths he utters proceed less from the facts established by the discoveries of the present century, than by the wavering intuitions of an impersonal existence. Amiel continually speaks of a world limited and adapted to his metaphysical conceptions. He forgets that we inhabit a universe composed of many worlds. In his world- which is small, on account of his inexperience- he has discovered several marvelous nooks of pure thought, but variety is wanting. In his garden are only flowers of his native soil,

Geneva, which was not yet freed from the specter of defunct Calvinism. Imagine a Carlyle always living in Edinburgh and you will have a Scotch Amiel. "La responsabilite est mon cauchemar invisible"- "Responsibility is my invisible nightmare." This is Calvinism hidden under a philosophical form; and this is why fully half of his Journal is composed of sermons and exhortations. Like Pascal, he is afraid of his own conscience, and his life is made miserable by fear. Today we doubt where Amiel and his predecessors trembled with terror. We of the present take life as it is, good and bad; for life, day by day, is already serious enough. Add to it the fear of the Beyond, and existence becomes insupportable.

Nothing is more interesting than to compare the reflections of Amiel on art with his reflections on morals. The first are nearly always strikingly just, clear, and clairvoyant; the second are generally confused and paradoxical. He attacks the character of Chateaubriand, and does his best to demolish the man; after which he extols his style, as if the man could be separated from his style! In speaking of Maine de Biran, the moralist of Geneva says: "Cette nature n'est qu'un des hommes qui sont en moi; c'est un de mes departements, ce n'est pas tout mon territoire, tout mon royaume interieur." Then he tells us why: "J'ai beaucoup plus vu d'hommes, de choses, de pays, de peuples et de livres; j'ai une plus grande masse d'experiences; en un mot, je me sens plus de culture, de richesse, d'etendue et de liberte, malgre mes lacunes, mes limites et mes faiblesses"- "This nature is only one of the men who are within me; it is one of my departments, not all my territory, all my interior kingdom. I have seen much more of men, of things, of countries, of peoples, and of books; I have a greater mass of experiences; in a word, I feel that I possess more culture, more riches, more compass and liberty, in spite of my wants, my limitations, and my weaknesses." And every word of this is quite true; he possessed more culture than Maine de Biran, but not enough to be liberated. Culture gives more liberty than does knowledge, and travel gives more knowledge than does scientific study. "Rien n'est melancolique et lassant comme ce Journal de Maine de Biran," he declares; "cette invariable monotonie de la reflexion qui se recommence sans fin enerve et decourage"- "Nothing is more melancholy and tiresome than this Journal of Maine de Biran; this interminable monotony of reflection, which recommences without end, enervates and discourages."

These moralists, taken singly, may be likened to a fortress which is supposed to be impregnable but whose commander is on the point of surrendering to the enemy for want of victuals; for they are hungry, they gnaw at their own vitals, and die of inanition.

If the Journal of Maine de Biran is, in Amiel's eyes, but "le voyage d'une fourmi qui s'accomplit dans les limites d'un champ, d'une taupe qui use ses jours dans la construction d'une taupiniere,"- "the voyage of an ant accomplished within the limits of a field, of a mole who spends his days in the construction of a mole-hill,"- that of Amiel is, in its turn, but the experiences of a pigeon that has left its roost in the belfry of a Calvinistic church to settle itself for a time in the turret of a German university.

Amiel is charming as a writer, interesting as an analyst, tiresome as a moralist. Moralists of this kind weary one another. Each sees in the others, incapacity, incertitude, vanity, and nothingness! The mirror which they mutually hold up to one another magnifies a hundred-fold the ephemerides of life, which become horrible monsters, inviting the unhappy *moi* to leap into the abyss of "predestination." The fright inspired by imaginative literature is but an effect of art; as such it interests, for the author is not a moralist, but an artist. We are fascinated by the artistic effect. There is something light and fantastic in the specters invoked by a Poe or a Hoffmann; follies there are which possess poetic charm, like that of Ophelia, singing, her hands filled with flowers; but the psychological maladies of the literary descendants of Pascal inspire a certain disquietude, a sentiment of uneasiness decidedly disagreeable. We have sniffed the fumes that arise from their inferno, and we flee in fear lest we also be asphyxiated. And each one of them must feel deep down within himself that he is playing a role in which much vanity is mixed with not a little hypocrisy.

All this is an atavic peculiarity of earlier superstition, the remains of the Dantesque in man's imagination- an element which is dissipated more and more every day; for we are no longer tormented by the fear of the Beyond; we are rather imbued with a sort of philosophical indifference in regard to these questions more puerile than practical, which surely terminate in disenchantment. Even the bourgeois, who reads his paper every morning, has become too shrewd to be long troubled by the nightmare of egoistic and vacillating ethics. The common-sense of the practical man of today leaves him neither time nor inclination for such futile speculation, though he be descended from the most implacable psychologist. The few thinkers of our day who have been brought up in the old disputatious school are to be pitied- they are no longer taken seriously.

What a subject for a study; the pathology of the typical moralists of all nationalities, from Pascal to Amiel!

CULTURE

I am inclined to agree with Francis Galton that education and environment produce only a small effect on the mind of anyone, and that most of our qualities are innate.

-Charles Darwin.

The supposition that culture can be attained by application and study is an error which has done incalculable mischief. Culture resembles genius in that it is born with one. Experience develops the faculties that we possess, just as the man of talent becomes a greater adept by application and practice, but experience adds little or nothing to temperament. We all know people who have spent a life-time in the vain hope of assimilating the culture of the best authors, composers, and artists. Yet how many can give an exact and critical account of anything they have seen, read, or heard? Ask yourself this question: How many of your friends, in so-called intellectual society, are qualified by nature to judge the best manifestation of art and thought in any form? You will find that A is a passably good judge of literature, but an ignoramus in regard to art; B is a fair judge of art, but no judge of good books; C is a lover of good music, but has little taste for art or literature, and so on. The man who professes a love for poetry, and who can gaze indifferently at a Turner, or listen unmoved to a score of Beethoven, is, after all, a dangerous person to deal with poetry; for what are the best poems but verbal music, and the best pictures but chromatic symphonies? A lack of any one intellectual quality tends to deprive all the others of their balance. A fanatic is a critic whose mind is fixed on one thing. Nor can he see that thing clearly, because he can neither conceive other symbols, nor experience other sensations. His knowledge of a thing is mechanical, and not artistic or intuitive.

MODERN MYSTICISM

This explains the inferiority of Meissonier's pictures; for in the world of art a man is a specialist because he lacks the large, free imagination which is akin to culture. The superficial mistake mere refinement for culture; but refinement is rarely more than an adjunct of the higher intelligence, denoting a delicate and fastidious nature, with the critical faculty chiefly shown in admiration of the obviously beautiful. Genius, which is nothing but culture made active, has a habit of revealing itself only to those who are intimate with its language and gestures. Its votaries know by certain mysterious and unwritten canons when they are in its presence. A marked originality of countenance and contour, which common minds often confound with eccentricity; a peculiar dream-expression, which the superficial mistake for stupidity; intermittent flashes of wit and wisdom, which the ignorant confuse with lack of stability; a surprising amount of moral courage, shown at unexpected moments- these are a few of the principal signs by which superlative minds may be recognized.

This explains the silent attitude of many gifted persons in the company of Strangers. They have learned the futility of frank speech on such occasions, and amuse themselves with talk politely called conversation. Reticence is the only refuge for a competent mind in a crowd, whether the crowd be large and cosmopolitan or limited and local.

In Macaulay's day the man with a powerful memory did all the talking. He held a dinner-table, or a drawing-room, like a pugilist, against all comers. A good memory was accepted as synonymous with wit, judgment, and even genius. In Johnson's time dogmatic assertion and self-assurance made the deepest impression. It was a sign of culture to talk at a man instead of with him. And since it is now considered an impertinence to say what one thinks in private, it is considered imperative to write what one thinks for the public. This is the only rational explanation of the multiplicity of books. Culture hides its personality in country cottages, foreign resorts, or remote islands of the High Seas, most thinking minds having taken to heart Victor Hugo's advice: "Ami, cache ta vie et repands ton esprit."

But there is a culture which is inactive and unproductive. It finds its sustenance in the appreciation that it bestows on the work of others. It is passive and unambitious. It is the invisible guard of militant and creative thought. Its possessors, scattered everywhere over the world, live in books, music, pictures, symbols, and a silence broken now and then by an exclamation of enthusiasm or a letter to some author or artist.

Intuitive knowledge, coupled with worldly experience, gives a natural leaning towards reticence. A certain indifference renders a man of much intuitive or worldly knowledge silent at the very moment when superficial wits are the most positive as well as the most triumphant. And the man who knows can well afford to sit still and let the one who thinks he knows play the "clever" one for the company. Even in intimate gatherings the poet and the artist know how much depends upon pleasant smiles, suave replies, and neutral opinions. Those who possess an intuitive mind are commonly misunderstood by their relatives and very often by their friends. There are few men and women of intellectual distinction who have not early in life been misjudged by their intimates. We are told that Robert Louis Stevenson, before he became celebrated, was considered eccentric, slovenly, and given to writing doggerel verse, which means that none suspected a cultured mind behind all this, as if fine clothes, conventional manners, and a solemn countenance were concomitants of intellect and talent.

Strict conformity to routine is one of the surest signs of intellectual mediocrity. The lower one goes in the scale of fashion, the more do people fear and avoid innovation, knowing that it requires a great title or talent for the successful introduction of new fads and fashions. The same thing happens in the world of the intellect. Only broad and independent minds can afford the luxury of originality. Thus it comes about that society is divided into two kinds of slaves- those who live in fear of conventional routine, and those who live in fear of being thought stupid.

A high intellectual development gives an assurance, a conviction, a mental repose, which sustain the individual under the most trying circumstances and most complicated conditions. Culture and personality are closely related.

THE ARTISTIC FACULTY IN LITERATURE

In literature the works not founded on proportion and harmony must, in the natural order of things, take a second place. Coleridge says: "Wherever there is a true rhythm and melody in words and sentences, there is also something good and profound in the meaning."

This harmony is the secret of logic, method, style, and wisdom. It pertains to the universal art of Shakespeare and Goethe- an art which contains the mathematical principles of fact and the metaphysical principles of reason, a union of the faculties and forces of observation and intuition. Thousands of us have, at times, grand ideas; the world is flooded with great thoughts, and even eloquence is a common thing; but the form, the music of real poetry is rare and priceless, and always will be. An artistic conception admits of no intermediary, it is either beyond or beneath criticism- if imperfect, no argument will make it perfect; if perfect, no praise will enhance its intrinsic worth. The mission of poetry and art is to be beautiful; but he who can add the most force and fervor to the greatest amount of beauty is the best artist, the best poet. Since philosophical systems are no longer tolerable, the mission of art, to thinking minds, is not to preach, but to give a spiritualized pleasure, to harmonize and charm. The most perfect poems are those which were written with an eye solely to the development of beauty; for it is the business of the poet to imagine, to see, to invent, but the artist must step in to put chaotic dreams and reveries into perfect form, dress them up, and send them out to shine among the grandees of the intellectual universe. Poetic inspirations possess certain characteristics with which the artist must know how to deal; the idea contained in Poe's Raven is a melancholy dream in black and white; anything else would have turned it into a farce instead of an exquisite fantasy. In Tennyson's Lotus Eater's we have a dream in pale yellow; to have added dashes of high coloring to this picture would have dissipated the central idea. Gray's Elegy is a reverie in which the dominant colors are those of the "sere and yellow leaf." Seven years were required to put the proper polish on this jewel, and the art here, as in all bits of perfect work, is completely hidden under the charm of its melancholy music. I can easily imagine the difficulties experienced by the poet in completing this poem owing to the almost impossible adjustment of tint and tone and the faultless harmony essential from beginning to end; a silent procession was set marching from the cradle to the grave, accompanied by music from lowing herds and distant church bells.

Poets, as a rule, are more favored in the gift of imagination, in the evolution of ideas, than in the ability to express them. Their most serious stumbling-block is the faculty of expression. Pains and patience will not give this faculty, but will aid it, develop it, and render it less laborious in time. I know of nothing in the whole range of art that can be acquired by practice except a certain mechanical facility. Sentiment, enthusiasm, grace, power, and style must all come into the world with us, as natural gifts that unite the mysticism of the mind with the magnetism of the individual. Rachel was taught to gesticulate and to pose in classical attitudes, but Nature alone could give her a lyrical voice and a lithesome figure. The greatest danger lies in the mistake made by young beginners, who expect to arrive at a plane of intellectual and artistic perfection by hard work alone.

The various spheres of intellectual adaptability are filled to overflowing by thousands who expect push and patience to supply the lack of Nature's gifts. They work and wait for years before the sad certainty dawns upon them that, in the domain of art, labor without talent is labor lost. All thought forced from the brain mechanically is without artistic value. In science, philosophy, politics, and religion, sincerity and enthusiasm are the most important factors, but in art and literature the form must be added to stamp sincerity with a flash of artistic light which shall reflect the poetic image in the magic-mirrors of time and memory. In reading certain pages of Thomas De Quincey one experiences the same sensations as when reading Milton, and none but a writer with the ear of a musician, the eye of an artist, and the soul of a poet, could have written the Confessions of an English Opium Eater. Here we have one of the greatest of all literary feats: a combination of music, color, and imagination, conceived and developed with faultless harmony. The idea, once captured, was never for a moment permitted to escape; then began a radiation of tinted rhetoric that shot out from all sides of the central impression, merging into a music expressive of every emotion of the soul- a perfect adjustment of the most delicate shades and meanings of art.

When writing attains the perfection shown by De Quincey it comes within the meaning of Buffon's saying: "The best prose is the best poetry."

It is a common expression that art, music, and literature are generally found together, but this is an error. They should be found together, but only in rare instances are they equally developed in the same mind. It is the lack of this unity which gives the world so many failures in the sphere of intellectualism. Had Michelangelo been less an architect or artist he would also have been less a poet and sculptor. Without an exception, the greatest men of genius have been those who possessed several faculties in the domain of art and thought, all equally developed. In the highest regions of intellectual achievement the maxim, "adhere to one thing if you wish to excel," has no significance. When we rise to that point where the generative process of inspiration begins, we cease to move within the limits of the art that tunes its melodies to one string; we are then in a world where the slightest emotion sets in movement the mystic instruments of thought and feeling, and wrests from the heart a thousand creations that descend on the world as miracles of poetry and wisdom. The condor that sits on the heights is king of the air; his sense of sight and sound, his marvelous speed, give him a power beyond all other creatures of space, and the fact is apparent that his swiftness is exactly in proportion to the immense height at which he soars; but as regards artistic enthusiasm. It requires a dexterous hand to manage a charger which, at the first sound of the clarion, rushes toward the center of confusion. Milton rode one of these chargers when he began Paradise Lost. He was ushered into the poetic war by the sound of every instrument known in the choir of the Muses; but he did not pause between the battles to let his Pegasus drink at the fountain of art. Milton possessed the faculties of music and imagination, but he often lacked harmonious arrangement, unity, and artistic judgment; he could not build like Dante, who possessed the triple faculty of art, music, and imagination, and who glided from one field of action to another with a harmony and unity that seem faultless.

Dante was not only a practical musician like Milton, but he was also a practical artist, and for these reasons when he visited Purgatory or Paradise a musician's ear heard every sound, and an artist's pencil sketched every scene. The works that strike us as inferior are those that emanate from minds devoid of one or more of the intellectual faculties, and it is not a difficult thing to tell just where a writer, an artist, or a musician has failed; certain signs, apparently trivial, show what faculty is lacking. With the same certainty the hand of the master can be seen in all work built on the basis of absolute beauty. This is the kind of work that will live and have its being, in spite of envious and malicious criticism; and every denial of a perfect piece of work only serves to enhance the fame of the workman. An artistic idea is analogous to a piece of money that has come down to us through centuries of mint-stamping, till it has passed through every country and clime, and from kings to presidents; the bit of metal is the same today, but the effigy is different; every time it passes through a new mint its form is changed. The only novelty an idea can have in our day is the manner of its dress. Strictly speaking, the creative faculty has little to do with ideas, since a hundred men may, and do, lay claim to the same thought; but the arrangement of ideas should be original with every mind of real ability. James Russell Lowell justly says: "The same thought uttered a thousand times is his at last who utters it best."

The world was never so hungry for sermons as for harmony and beauty in what it sees, hears, and reads. What gives to the Greek statue that indefinable air of artistic perfection? The secret lies in the neutrality of repose. It is there to be taken for what it is- a perfect conception of an idea without a suggestion of intellectual antagonism. The moment we begin to sermonize we sever the delicate thread that binds the sense of beauty to that of passive harmony. There is less art shown in the writing of novels than in any other phase of literature, the novel being of such easy access to people with a theory or a system. George Eliot would have shown herself in her books the consummate artist which Nature intended her to be, had she not exaggerated on the side of psychological analysis; when she overcame this temptation her work flashed with the impersonal brilliancy of a well-cut jewel. In such moments her thought was like the embodiment of a perfect rose, complete in form and fragrance, to be appropriated alike by the ignorant and the cultured. Goethe made a similar blunder in *Wilhelm Meister,* Victor Hugo in *Les Miserables*, Tolstoy in *Anna Karenina,* George Sand in *Consuelo*, to mention but a few instances out of hundreds.

That so great an artist as Goethe should give us a long-winded treatise on horticulture in a work dealing with philosophy, love, and romance, that Victor Hugo should wear us out with interminable details about the sewers of Paris in a novel of exciting romance, are more proofs of the uncertain judgment of many of the greatest novelists. The value of a work diminishes exactly in proportion as the author seeks to establish an ethical system of his own. Perhaps the best safeguard against proselytizing in literature is to rest quietly on impartial ground, where one's pet theories may slumber whilst imagination and reason wander as free as the air from Daphne's grove to the Delphian oracle. This is the charm which renders a thing of beauty a joy for ever, and it would not be a perpetual joy if it conflicted with the judgment of the majority of cultured minds. The brand of artistic fate is burned into the vitals of every poem or book as it falls from the hands of the author, long before it is read by the public. There is no escape; before the last drop of ink has dried on the last page of your brain's production your efforts have been weighed in the balance by that impartial and classical jury known as the Nine Muses, against whose judgment the fool has no appeal by tears, nor the tyrant by treaty.

One of the most infallible signs of permanent worth appears to revolve on an axis of time and trouble- time, to ripen and polish; suffering, both mental and physical, to prepare the soil, to sift illusions from realities, to create a smoldering fire of feeling and sincerity which should never fall below a certain temperature. Some authors wait in misery ten, others, like Balzac, twenty years, before they pierce the layer of public prejudice; and the patience they possess is taxed according to the age and country in which they live. Some one has defined genius as the gift of patience, but patience without a consciousness of superiority would mean nothing. It is impossible to do perfect work of any kind without a consciousness that it can be done in a manner above the average. We may search in vain for an instance where a man of genius has taken up a special line of work without a conviction that the task to be accomplished will be done better by him than by anyone else. Just in proportion as we descend in the scale of talent, in the various degrees of intellectual endowment, the number of those who are doubtful of their work increases. A man who has spent the best part of his life in the school of experience and discipline is not afraid, if the opportunity occurs, to declare his opinions; he will not be swayed by the fear of contradiction, will not stop to ask permission to deliver his message. But this does not mean that the number of those who believe they were born to move the world is decreasing; there never was a time when so many crude works, in every sphere of art, have received the encomiums that only the productions of the most gifted intellects deserve. The realistic novel can be produced by one or more persons in every town. The facts are there before you- marriages, births, divorces, feasts, and funerals; knead them, like dough for a dumpling, season the lump with the spice of passion, and the crude mass, sodden and indigestible, is ready for the market. Writers who spend their time in this way may be divided into two classes- those who write for money, and those who write for enduring fame. The former sometimes achieve their desire, whilst the latter are doomed to that inexorable and oft-repeated failure known to those who labor under the hallucinations that spring from chronic ignorance, and which, in most cases, cling to the victim till death.

In Germany there used to be a saying that the world has known but three men of genius- Homer, Shakespeare, and Goethe; the English and the French are much less restricted in the use of the title; it is left for the Americans to use that word- significant of universal talent and intelligence- in connection with clever mechanics and inventors, politicians, singers, actors, etc. The world does not stop to meditate on the vast distinction between intellectual attainment and genius. Certainly, talented people must come into the world with an uncommon share of brain-power and a certain amount of culture which cannot be acquired; but as to genius, there is an impassable gulf between it and everything else. While infinite pains may develop talent, it is only connected with genius by conditional ties. The moment we leave the boundaries of talent we enter a country where the laws and the language differ as widely from those of the land we have just left as the scenes and sentiments of London differ from those of Paris. Every man of originality is an alien even in his own country until one by one friends and acquaintances appear who are familiar with his mode of thought. Years are spent in studying the language of a new genius, and, as we do not appreciate the height of a mountain until we climb its foot-hills, so we cannot grasp the true measure of a man of genius until we approach his plane of culture; it often happens, however, that before we reach this plane the man himself slips away from us into the regions of the Infinite. Little faith can be placed in the possibility of perfect impromptu productions where the length of the work is to be considered. The lightning thought which illuminates the imagination rarely gives more than a hint at the form, except in aphorisms, short sentences, and lines that stand out clear, strong, and musical from the first conception. Emerson's essays are a brilliant example of the inharmonious construction of a mass of powerful and original thought in a single page or chapter. It is apparent that each sentence was a flash of vivid imagination combined with philosophical force, but his aphorisms, perfect in themselves when taken singly, lack consecutive unity. His thoughts, while containing all the freshness and vigor of impromptu illumination, are strung together like finely cut jewels, regardless of size or color. We often hear of some new work, the style of which, we are told, clothes the vulgar motive of the story in illusive idealism. Such a feat is impossible. When Zola began a history of brutal characters his pen could not, if it would, depict a series of idealistic portraits. There never was, and never will be, a scientific work written in the style of *The Waverley Novels* or *La Comedie Humaine*. Without an exception, the true measure of artistic excellence is shown in the work of every author who is at liberty to write according to his inclinations. No discussion or contradiction can obscure the truth of this axiom. The moment a poet or a writer feels that he is independent he will express himself in his best and most congenial vein; and it is in this light that we are bound to judge the true tastes, inclinations, and powers of every poet, writer, and artist whose works are given to the world.

THE END

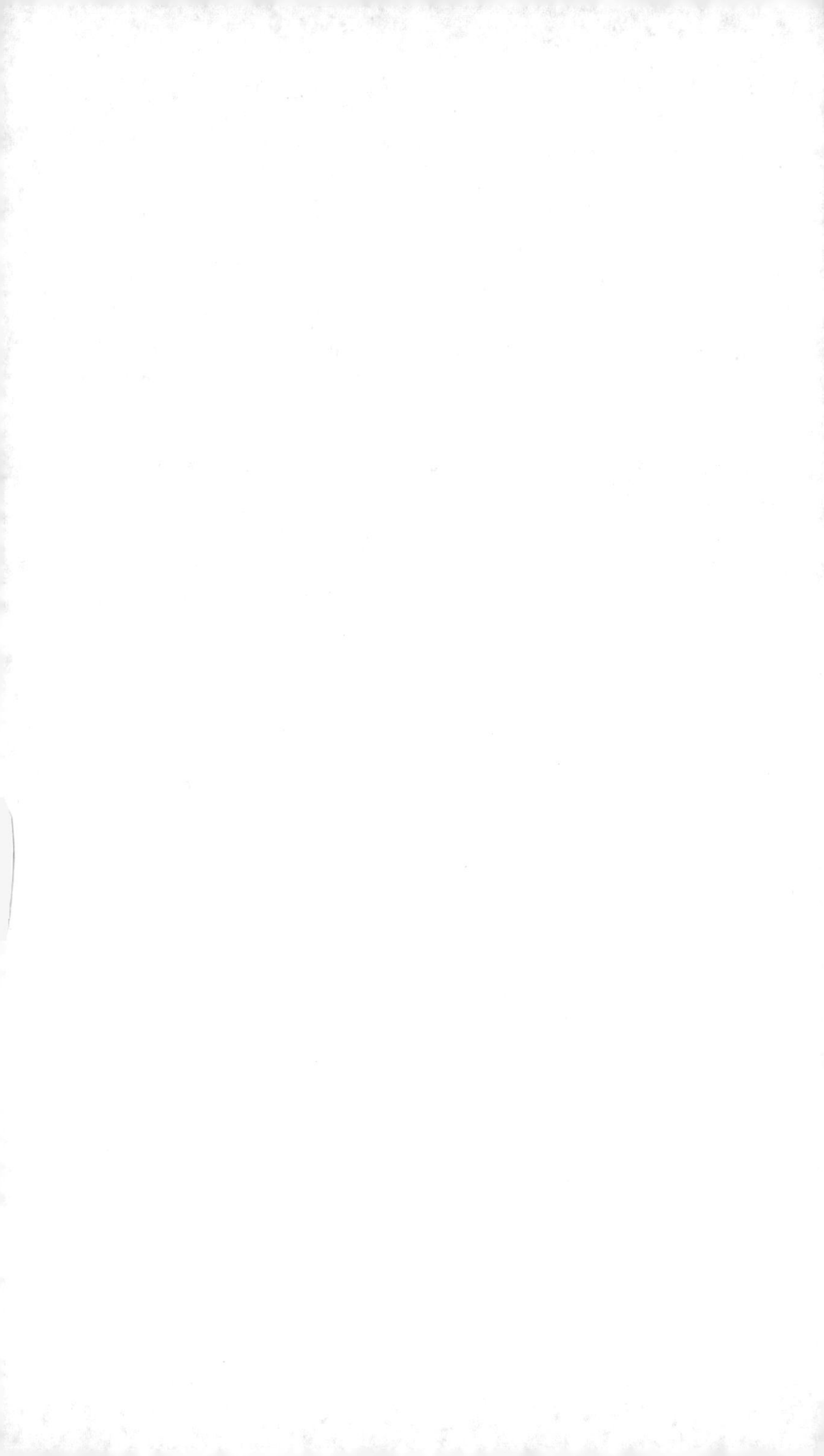